THOUGHT CATALOG BOOKS

Beyond Depression

Beyond Depression

Essays About Feeling Low, Feeling Stuck, And Finding Healing

THOUGHT CATALOG

THOUGHT CATALOG BOOKS

Brooklyn

THOUGHT CATALOG BOOKS

Copyright © 2016 by The Thought & Expression Co.

All rights reserved. Published by Thought Catalog Books, a division of The Thought & Expression Co., Williamsburg, Brooklyn. Founded in 2010, Thought Catalog is a website and imprint dedicated to your ideas and stories. We publish fiction and non-fiction from emerging and established writers across all genres. For general information and submissions: manuscripts@thoughtcatalog.com.

First edition, 2016

ISBN 978-1540557155

10 9 8 7 6 5 4 3 2 1

Cover photography by © Volkan Olmez

Contents

1

Nothing About My Depression Is 'Haunting' Or 'Beautiful,' Everything About It Is Awful

Katie Mather

I'm not quite sure when the meeting was to decide that depression was the première mental illness to glamorize by mentally healthy people, but I was certainly not invited.

When I was a sophomore in college, I was officially diagnosed with depression. Although, after one of my school's counselors (who honestly might've actually been a psych student who was, like, only four years older than me—I think he got assigned to me by accident) read me the symptoms, I suspected that I had been depressed since the early years of high school.

Since then, depression is now a very reluctantly accepted part of my life. It's ingrained into my personality and my actions. It influences my thoughts, feelings, and decisions.

Which is why online content and people who glorify depression as ~*~moodiness~*~ or mysteriousness or enviable darkness or *whatever* absolutely astound me.

Because I have been to the depths of hell before with my good buddies, Depression and Anxiety, and, frankly, I did *naht* see any of those people down there helping me.

Depression isn't beautiful. It's ugly. It's hideous to the point that when you're taken over by it, people turn away. And nobody ignores beauty.

"Haunting" oversimplifies the complete travesty that depression wreaks in almost every aspect of your life. Depression isn't "difficult to ignore," *holy shit*, no: depression makes it difficult to think about anything else. Depression becomes you.

Depression is something you want to hide—you stuff it down your throat as you frantically try to find a distraction, until that point when everything bubbles up and you barely want to exist anymore.

Depression is losing will because you can't conjure up a good enough reason to do anything.

Depression is failing to find a reason to want to be conscious and to get out of bed.

Depression is not washing your hair for days. It's not brushing your teeth. It's wearing unclean clothes.

Depression is eating. It's eating so many Strawberry Pop-Tarts in one sitting, you feel heavy and slow. It's not eating for days, and feeling empty and hollow. It's both, it's over and over again, it never stops.

Depression is sleep. Too much, and way too little. You're always tired, and not from the lack of sleep; you're a weird, unknown type of exhaustion that sneaks into your life and somehow, without you noticing, becomes part of who you are.

Depression is constantly apologizing to people you love for who you are.

What part of this is beautiful? What part of this is mysterious and brooding and exciting to be around?

If you want to use simplified language to talk about depression—language that barely scratches the surface—it's not beautiful or haunting. It's awful.

2

15 Struggles People Who Bottle Up Their Feelings Understand

Christopher Hudspeth

1. It may be exhausting but you can put on Oscar-worthy acting performances for days, weeks or even months at a time, pretending to be okay with people and things that are actually stressing you out & driving you crazy. You're basically a super dedicated, unpaid method actor.

2. Giving attitude here and there is a survival mechanism you use to avoid exploding. It's a way of slightly sedating a potential blow up temporarily. Think of it like slowly unscrewing the cap of a soda so the carbonation doesn't cause a massive, fizzy mess and overflow out of the bottle.

3. Thinking that your feelings are foreign to everyone else. When you see yourself as somewhat of a Martian, it's easy to refrain from expressing what's inside because you're fairly certain nobody wouldn't understand anyway.

4. In modern dating, there are a lot of games being played, which can lead people to mistake your lack of feelings being expressed for an attempt at the popular "I bet I can care less than you do" shenanigans.

5. The silent treatment isn't something you intend to use childishly, but more to get your point across. Silence is like an uncomfortable comfort zone for you to hold things in but also make it clear that you're not thrilled with someone.

6. Eventually, you'll blow up. It's inevitable. Probably randomly, all of those feelings will come out at once, and you'll have the friendliness of a possessed person in the midst of an exorcism.

7. When you're in a relationship and don't want to hurt your partner's feelings, you'll hold things in as an unspoken favor, saving them from your potentially upsetting honest thoughts.

8. A common way to validate your holding things in is by telling yourself that they'll slowly expire or you can last bottling 'em up until the cause of them passes. You're probably wrong, but it's a great excuse in the moment.

9. Innocent bystanders and undeserving individuals are at risk when you finally reach your boiling point. They aren't the cause of your frustration, but get the brunt of the punishment. For example, one of your co-workers is excessively rude to you for three months straight and you deal with it, then one day another co-worker asks to borrow your stapler and you're like, "SERIOUSLY??! SURE, COME OVER HERE TO USE MY STAPLER BECAUSE IT'S SO HARD TO KEEP TRACK OF YOUR OWN OFFICE SUPPLIES AND I'M THE

ONLY ONE WITH A DAMN STAPLER AROUND HERE. STAPLE AWAY, DUDE. LAST TIME I CHECKED I'M NOT AN OFFICE DEPOT. THE LAKERS DON'T PLAY BASKET-BALL INSIDE OF ME SO I'M NOT THE STAPLES CEN-TER! WHY DOESN'T DAD EVEN CARE ENOUGH TO CALL?... I mean...Whatever, just use the stapler and go away."

10. Those rare instances where you do pour your heart out to someone had better go well, otherwise you'll be devastated and further convinced that it's just easier to say absolutely nothing about how you feel for the foreseeable future.

11. You understand how different opinions & feelings are. You may speak your mind and share your views, but when it comes to feelings you'll hold off.

12. There's a slight fear of consuming too much alcohol because that liquid courage could mean a whole lot of brutal, frustrated honesty coming out. Will you snap and say too much? Will you hurt feelings and ruin friendships? Find out next drink on, *Uh-oh It's About To Go Down!*

13. Beating yourself up even further inside because you know that you're bottling toxic sentiments up and need to speak your mind, but have failed to do so. Now not only are you mad at the world, but you're shaming and being hard on yourself.

14. After spending so much time biting your tongue and holding back for the sake of others that you're a mess inside, when someone finally asks you, "How are things going?" or

"Is everything okay?" you're overcome with all of the feels and want to burst into tears (and probably be hugged). You've bottled up an abundance of emotions and they just unscrewed the cap. You might be able to muster up a trembling "I'm fine" and escape before the waterworks begin, but this only ends with you crying, whether it be on their shoulder or in private.

15. Deep down you understand that life is too short to not tell people how you feel, and there's a constant battle within to improve on it. New Year's resolution? *I'm going to be more open with people.* Randomly motivated to change? *I'm going to be more open with people.* It's something you strive for, but ironically it's much easier for you to **say** than do.

3

Explaining Depression To Someone Who Isn't Depressed

Nikita Gill

Have you ever felt hunted inside your own head?

Like a predator is loose in there, stalking you like prey?

Like there is a thing inside of your mind, a dark, dangerous, devious thing and it is stalking you. Your mind, a forest of beautiful trees and alive with birds and wild things alike, is eerily silent, a shroud of night covering it like a blanket on a too hot night—this is what suffocating is. But on the outside, you are breathing in oxygen as you always do. Your mind has sliced itself away from your body, and you have no control over what happens in there anymore. But you are still in this forest. You are alive in there...and there is a thing, an evil thing stalking you.

It starts to set parts of your head aflame, a forest fire threatening to take over you as it tries to smoke you out of your own head. Panicked, you are running, knowing you are being hunted, you are being chased, and you do not even know what the thing that is hunting you looks like. If you could give this fear, this terror a name, it would be better—a lion, a tiger, a shark, a thing that wants your blood and meat, nothing else from you, but this goes deeper. This thing wants every peaceful part of your mind. This thing wants to set you on fire and watch you burn, laugh at your ashes and then bring you to life so it can do it again. Or worse, swallow you whole and keep you in an abyss of eternal sadness inside your own head.

You are running inside the labyrinth of your mind, as it grows more and more complex, away from the thing, yet drawing closer to it, you can smell it the way it grows closer to you with ease. It doesn't even need to run. Somewhere in the distance in the hot dusty trail within this maze of a forest, you see the house, the place inside your head where you keep the softest, kindest memories. This is where you keep your cushions for when life throws you hard against the wall and you are lying bleeding on the floor. This is the place you must go to… Singed by the flames, you run faster and faster, the thing hot on yours heels until with all the strength you ever had, you throw yourself into this safe space with all the energy you have left within you and slam the door.

Panting, exhausted, you collapse, for the first time, feeling the rush of relief since it started its hunt. In here, you do not feel like prey. In here, you are safe. Until you open your eyes when you hear the breathing so close to you, the stink of its breath. It's in here with you, and your eyes open wide as you realize too late…it has devoured your already, all of you now belongs to it. And all that is left is darkness.

This is what depression feels like. This is what it means when someone says they have depression. This is what depressed people mean when they say they feel devoured by sadness, unable to escape the pain inside their own heads.

Have you ever felt hunted inside your own head?

If not…I envy you your good fortune. But please do not be unkind when I tell you about the monster, the predator that lives inside my head.

4

10 Confessions Of Someone With Depression

Ella Ceron

1. There's a difference between sadness and depression, and though that doesn't take away from a diagnosis, it is empowering as a distinction.

Though you may *feel* depressed, a person who has depression is not *always* a "depressed person," in whatever way—hyperbolic or otherwise—that phrase has come to mean. I was diagnosed with clinical depression, anxiety, and obsessive tendencies when I was a teenager, but I probably exhibited symptoms of depression long before that. Still, I didn't understand why sometimes I would just feel sad, and sometimes I'd suddenly just find everything to be entirely too much and shut off from the rest of the world at the drop of a hat. Those moments were stronger than your run-of-the-mill sadness. Slowly, you learn to distinguish what is just feeling sad and what is depression, and you begin to strategize when it comes to seeing each one through.

2. One of the most useful strategies I've found, plain and simple: make it a point to laugh every day.

Especially on the days when things just feel godawful and sad and like there is nothing really worth laughing about, I force myself to laugh—and to make myself laugh if I can. I think up little jokes, I talk to friends who I think are funny, I watch a show I really love, anything to just remind myself that you can be sad and laugh in the same day, and even at the same time. Your depression is only one facet of you, no matter how much it may loom over you and cloud the rest of your emotions, but forcing a little bit of laughter in daily works wonders. (Honestly, it's when I'm saddest that I tend to make the *most* jokes. It provides a good distraction).

3. Still, there are some days when things just hurt. That's nothing to run away from. That's something to embrace as—wait for it—normal.

The expectation that life is supposed to be breezy all the time is dangerous. It's not breezy all the time, even to the most well-adjusted individual. Expecting life to always be easy leads you further down the rabbit hole of feeling terrible when you're trying to force yourself to be better, to be less depressed, to just "snap out of it." Sometimes, you can't. Often, you shouldn't.

My bad hours and days happen most when I'm forcing myself to take a break and can't escape my own thoughts and fears and anxieties with work or friends. Things will just hurt, and

I'll find myself wondering if people on the subway know that the girl sitting next to them is fighting off a panic attack—*they have to know, right? Oh god it's so obvious* is usually my train of thought—or I'll sit in the shower and just let the water run over my body, or I'll listen to sad music and just cry. Because you can't always escape those emotions. Every now and again, it just hurts for no reason at all, and it becomes tiring to try to outrun the heaviness of it all. Sometimes you just have to feel it.

4. I know a bad day doesn't mean a bad life. We all know that. Maybe it's time to learn that a bad month or a bad few years or a bad experience or relationship doesn't either.

I know I have a good life, filled with amazing friends and a wonderful family. I genuinely love my job (and a lot of people, with or without depression, don't always feel that way about their jobs, so I know that makes me a little weird in its own merit). I have tons of things to be thankful for, and I am thankful for them.

My brain is just wired a little differently—whether it's a chemical imbalance or a rocky adolescence or just too much emotion zooming around my head is up for debate. It's probably a combination of the three, and none of those hold any bearing on how I value the world I've made for myself. It's just an entirely different matter I'm dealing with. You can have a wonderful life and still be depressed. The latter doesn't mean you're any less grateful for the former.

5. I know I am lucky that my depression is, for the most part, manageable. It really can be.

Most forms of depression are, and whether that is due to medication, therapy, exercise, or a combination of those or anything else varies from person to person. I hated the way medication made me feel, and I know that was probably a matter of not finding the proper medication or dosage, but after cycling on and off more pills than I care to remember, I had to make the decision that I didn't want to send my body through any more chemical roller coasters in the hopes of finding what might work for me. I began running and eating a plant-based diet instead, and that works for me. Some people find the right dosage on the first try, if medication is what they want. Some people aren't so lucky, and they do try multiple prescriptions before finding the right thing. A lot of people go to therapy. Some people turn to exercise, or other methods of sorting their brains out. No one choice is better than the other. No one coping mechanism is for more "serious" or "mild" cases of depression than the other, and no one prescription is a cure-all for every form of depression. We're each all trying to deal in our own way, and however that way is made manageable is the way you ought to go.

6. ...You know the dementors in *Harry Potter?* I wish those were real creatures.

Really, I do. Explaining away something with spectral, undead, happiness-feeding evil creatures that suck your soul out of your body and leave you as a dark shell is A) a pretty accurate description for depression anyway, and B) sounds a lot cooler than synapses misfiring and needing to get some endorphins pumping in my brain again. Also, I'd like an excuse to eat chocolate like that.

7. If I let you know I'm feeling depressed, I'm genuinely not trying to drag you down with me.

If anything, knowing that another person I love and care about feels affected by a mood that, for the most part, I largely can't help is enough to make me feel guilty on top of the myriad of emotions I'm already sorting through. It's not a good feeling. I'm not asking you to try to "fix" me, or to take on the burden of my sadness—I wouldn't wish that on anyone. Letting someone know you're depressed is not a cry for help—it's just a method of reaching out and hopefully feeling less alone.

8. There are entire days where you feel like a completely normal human being—whatever that is.

And there are days when it feels like winter is endless and everything is just overwhelmingly heavy, but talking about those days feels like dwelling. You have to sift through them, of course, but sometimes it helps to just enjoy the good days for what they are. Understanding why they're good sort of defeats the point—sometimes you just have to revel in the fact that you feel *good*. Analyzing it would only put stress on it, and I imagine that sometimes people who don't have depression aren't all that consumed with breaking down the concept as to why they're happy—they just are, in that moment. And someone who has depression often needs to cling that much more tightly to the good days and enjoy them for what they are.

9. You don't have to look like the stereotypical "sad person" to have depression.

After all, tons of really successful people—including comedians, who always seem to be the antithesis of what people imagine depression to look like—have had depression. Some of them beat it, some of them cope with it, and some of them unfortunately don't. You never know what kind of battle someone is facing. Sometimes, even putting that much more effort into how you look or how you present yourself can keep your demons at bay, if only for a few hours or a day. If that is all you need to get through another moment in the here and now, then that will serve as enough. Beautiful things often come from the most tortured places, and making art and laughter and culture from a place of depression is no different.

10. I don't want you to treat me like I'm fragile. This isn't about being "lesser" for experiencing a human condition. This is about being honest about something that a lot of people deal with.

And I don't always need to talk about the stuff that's on my mind, but sometimes, it does help to sort things out. But there is a difference between going to a friend for commiseration, and seeking out therapy, and most people with depression know that it's unwise and even a little unsafe to treat a friend as a therapist. (This is why though I've been in therapy for over a decade, I can't provide any more insight than my own, whatever that is worth in the scope of someone else feeling less alone.) But if I tell you that I'm feeling depressed, I don't want you to tiptoe around me. I'm just letting you know so that you understand that whatever it is that is dragging me down isn't on you. That's not your burden to bear. And even your just being around me and treating me like I'm still just another normal human being with a correctly calibrated emotional spectrum helps. Treat me like I'm me, not like I'm going to shatter at every moment. That helps more than you could ever know.

5

This Is What Depression Really Looks Like

Ari Eastman

Depression doesn't just look like a Cymbalta commercial.

To be honest, I've always hated those stupid commercials. Every damn one with just slightly different versions of the same character: the unshaven lump of a man who can barely muster up the energy to get out of bed. He's the epitome of lifeless, a shell of a human being.

But hold up, have no fear! He pops that glorious pill and cheery music begins to crescendo. Like magic, he remembers how to brush his hair! He shaves! He's not wearing a stained sweatshirt! Oh happy day! He's done it!!!

But that's not how depression is. It can be. Sometimes, depression does look a lot like not being able to get out of bed or face the day. But it's so much more. There isn't one way depression is supposed to look, one identity you can pin to depression. It doesn't hit only a certain demographic. Depression is like cancer, heart disease, addiction, etc. It's a disease that doesn't care who you are. It just doesn't care.

I don't know how to really describe depression. I really try. I've tried for most of my life to put it into words. Funny thing that happens when you're a writer, you're not sure how to write about the one thing you want to the most. Maybe that's not very funny at all, actually.

Instead, I usually default to a joke. My anxiety and depression were always so much a part of my personality, I learned how to make it seem like part of my humor. It was this potentially lovable quirk, "Oh Ari, she gets so worried about things, but she's also a goofball! What a kook!" Zooey Deschanel blew up and I gotta say, it just further helped cement my depression never seeming too serious. This *kinda-nervous-awkward-but-still-obviously-functions-as-a-human-being* type person was okay for me to embrace. I just had to keep joking. I had to keep it light and airy. Quirky, neurotic, but acceptably neurotic.

Because nobody wants to hear stories of 10 year old Ari, staring at her ceiling, fighting insomnia with this unshakable feeling of impending doom. That's not fun. That's not light and airy. Nobody wants a translation of the thoughts I don't say out loud. Nobody wants to know my obsession with isolation. I crave solitude in a way that I'm not always sure is healthy.

Who wants to hear that shit? It's suddenly not the joke anymore. I'm not the entertainer anymore, making people laugh and letting everyone off the hook. I do whatever I can to ease discomfort. I don't want people to be burdened with my brain. So I'll deflect, I'll refer to Zoloft as my boyfriend but laugh after, so it's okay. Right? It's okay. I'm laughing, so I'm *okay*.

I don't usually look like the characters in Cymbalta commercials. I laugh a lot. And nothing gives me the same kind of high as making others laugh too. I am the goofball. I am the neurotic-still-functioning person you all think. Most people who get to know me actually say I'm pretty much the same on the internet as I am in person. I really am actually happy quite often. I enjoy the fuck out of life so much of the time. But depression exists within me too. It's there. It's been there for so long, I can't remember a time without it. And though it continues to be a journey, I've accepted it. I've come to terms with it.

Depression doesn't look like one thing. So don't expect it to. You aren't supposed to be one thing.

6

19 Of The Best Quotes That Perfectly Explain What Depression Feels Like

Koty Neelis

1. "I didn't want to wake up. I was having a much better time asleep. And that's really sad. It was almost like a reverse nightmare, like when you wake up from a nightmare you're so relieved. I woke up into a nightmare."

—**Ned Vizzini,** *It's Kind Of A Funny Story*

2. "The so-called 'psychotically depressed' person who tries to kill herself doesn't do so out of quote 'hopelessness' or any abstract conviction that life's assets and debits do not square. And surely not because death seems suddenly appealing. The person in whom Its invisible agony reaches a certain unendurable level will kill herself the same way a trapped person will eventually jump from the window of a burning high-rise. Make no mistake about people who leap from burning windows. Their terror of falling from a great height is still just as great as it would be for you or me standing speculatively at

the same window just checking out the view; i.e. the fear of falling remains a constant. The variable here is the other terror, the fire's flames: when the flames get close enough, falling to death becomes the slightly less terrible of two terrors. It's not desiring the fall; it's terror of the flames. And yet nobody down on the sidewalk, looking up and yelling 'Don't!' and 'Hang on!', can understand the jump. Not really. You'd have to have personally been trapped and felt flames to really understand a terror way beyond falling."

—**David Foster Wallace**

3. "Passion makes a person stop eating, sleeping, working, feeling at peace. A lot of people are frightened because, when it appears, it demolishes all the old things it finds in its path.

No one wants their life thrown into chaos. That is why a lot of people keep that threat under control and are somehow capable of sustaining a house or a structure that is already rotten. They are the engineers of the superseded.

Other people think exactly the opposite: they surrender themselves without a second thought, hoping to find in passion the solutions to all their problems. They make the other person responsible for their happiness and blame them for their possible unhappiness. They are either euphoric because something marvelous has happened or depressed because something unexpected has just ruined everything.

Keeping passion at bay or surrendering blindly to it—which of these two attitudes is the least destructive?

I don't know."

—**Paulo Coelho**

4. "Some friends don't understand this. They don't understand how desperate I am to have someone say, I love you and I support you just the way you are because you're wonderful just the way you are. They don't understand that I can't remember anyone ever saying that to me. I am so demanding and difficult for my friends because I want to crumble and fall apart before them so that they will love me even though I am no fun, lying in bed, crying all the time, not moving. Depression is all about If you loved me you would."

—**Elizabeth Wurtzel**, *Prozac Nation*

5. "There is no point treating a depressed person as though she were just feeling sad, saying, 'There now, hang on, you'll get over it.' Sadness is more or less like a head cold—with patience, it passes. Depression is like cancer."

—**Barbara Kingsolver**, *The Bean Trees*

6. "When you're surrounded by all these people, it can be lonelier than when you're by yourself. You can be in a huge crowd, but if you don't feel like you can trust anyone or talk to anybody, you feel like you're really alone."

—**Fiona Apple**

7. "If you know someone who's depressed, please resolve never to ask them why. Depression isn't a straightforward response to a bad situation; depression just is, like the weather.

Try to understand the blackness, lethargy, hopelessness, and loneliness they're going through. Be there for them when they come through the other side. It's hard to be a friend to someone who's depressed, but it is one of the kindest, noblest, and best things you will ever do."

—**Stephen Fry**

8. "I don't want to see anyone. I lie in the bedroom with the curtains drawn and nothingness washing over me like a sluggish wave. Whatever is happening to me is my own fault. I have done something wrong, something so huge I can't even see it, something that's drowning me. I am inadequate and stupid, without worth. I might as well be dead."

—**Margaret Atwood**, *Cat's Eye*

9. "I'll never forget how the depression and loneliness felt good and bad at the same time. Still does."

—**Henry Rollins**, *The Portable Henry Rollins*

10. "I was drawn to all the wrong things: I liked to drink, I was lazy, I didn't have a god, politics, ideas, ideals. I was settled into nothingness; a kind of non-being, and I accepted it. I didn't make for an interesting person. I didn't want to be interesting, it was too hard. What I really wanted was only a soft, hazy space to live in, and to be left alone."

—**Charles Bukowski**

11. "Others imply that they know what it is like to be depressed because they have gone through a divorce, lost a job, or broken up with someone. But these experiences carry with them feelings. Depression, instead, is flat, hollow, and unendurable. It is also tiresome. People cannot abide being around you when you are depressed. They might think that they ought to, and they might even try, but you know and they know that you are tedious beyond belief: you are irritable and paranoid and humorless and lifeless and critical and demanding and no reassurance is ever enough. You're frightened, and you're frightening, and you're "not at all like yourself but will be soon," but you know you won't."

—**Kay Redfield Jamison**, *An Unquiet Mind: A Memoir Of Moods And Madness*

12. "You say you're 'depressed'—all I see is resilience. You are allowed to feel messed up and inside out. It doesn't mean you're defective—it just means you're human."

—**David Mitchell**, *Cloud Atlas*

13. "He: What's the matter with you?

Me: Nothing.

Nothing was slowly clotting my arteries. Nothing slowly numbing my soul. Caught by nothing, saying nothing, nothingness becomes me. When I am nothing they will say surprised in the way that they are forever surprised, "but there was nothing the matter with her."

—**Jeanette Winterson**, *Gut Symmetries*

14. "Depression is the most unpleasant thing I have ever experienced… It is that absence of being able to envisage that you will ever be cheerful again. The absence of hope. That very deadened feeling, which is so very different from feeling sad. Sad hurts but it's a healthy feeling. It is a necessary thing to feel. Depression is very different."

—J.K. Rowling

15. "Depression is like a bruise that never goes away. A bruise in your mind. You just got to be careful not to touch it where it hurts. It's always there, though."

—Jeffrey Eugenides, *The Marriage Plot*

16. "Depression presents itself as a realism regarding the rottenness of the world in general and the rottenness of your life in particular. But the realism is merely a mask for depression's actual essence, which is an overwhelming estrangement from humanity. The more persuaded you are of your unique access to the rottenness, the more afraid you become of engaging with the world; and the less you engage with the world, the more perfidiously happy-faced the rest of humanity seems for continuing to engage with it."

—Jonathan Franzen, *How To Be Alone*

17. "I couldn't be with people and I didn't want to be alone. Suddenly my perspective whooshed and I was far out in space, watching the world. I could see millions and millions of people, all slotted into their lives; then I could see me—I'd lost my place in the universe. It had closed up and there was nowhere for me to be. I was more lost than I had known it was possible for any human being to be."

—**Marian Keyes**, *Anybody Out There?*

18. "Is there no way out the mind?"

—**Sylvia Plath**, *The Bell Jar*

19. "So why am I depressed? That's the million-dollar question, baby, the Tootsie Roll question; not even the owl knows the answer to that one. I don't know either. All I know is the chronology."

—**Ned Vizzini**, *It's Kind Of A Funny Story*

7

What It's Really Like To Live With High Functioning Depression

Sarah Elizabeth Jones

What is it like to be depressed but high functioning? It is fucking terrible. When you tell people you are depressed, they don't always believe you. When you find yourself finally comfortable enough with someone to tell them exactly, and not the carefully fabricated lie you had been trying to live, but exactly how you feel and they tell you it is too much for them it actually feels like clutching glass in both hands. There is no word for someone who suffers from depression. We are not Depressists or Depressionics; we have no title for the completely debilitating mental state of our core. Owning up to depression while trying to remain optimistic and cheerful like everyone tells you to do is mutually exclusive. They tell you not to bottle up your emotions, but when you try to release the carbonated gasses from your head you are told to shut it down.

The problem with being depressed but high functioning means that your friends, family, and coworkers all have a certain expectation from you. Some people may even envy you, falsely thinking your life is grand and beautiful like an Instagram at face value.

That is what being depressed but happy feels like, whatever void Instagram is. It is pretty and filtered and not the truth.

We have all come to accept that our social media lives are not our real lives, but we put a lot of effort into crafting a world in which we get to live out the lives we want. I packed up my things, quit my job, and moved to Australia with my best friend. I posted photos of the time I fed wild dolphins from the side of a boat, and of how silly adjusting to an accent was, and of my new, hot Australian boyfriend. I really did those things, I had those experiences and in those small moments I did feel some elation close to bliss. I could sit on the sand and look out at the ocean and try to describe to myself what color I was seeing because I hadn't seen it before. The ocean was blue and green and gold and red all at the same time. I had moments of serenity and calm and complete happiness. I have a memory of sitting on said boyfriend's couch watching David Attenborough documentaries with my legs curled over his and my head in the crook of his neck and shoulder and I experienced perfection. True, honest, perfection. He heard every word I said and he laughed every time I tried to be funny and he made my body feel lighter than air. We were a bit wild and unencumbered.

However, even in that beautiful, picturesque moment, I was

depressed. Even when I was feeling like I was falling in love, I was still in fact falling. I was questioning. I was fearful. I was clinging to the moment, so afraid of the future. We broke up so shortly after that, for many reasons of which neither of us hold it against the other. We were symptoms of "bad timing." I still hold my very attractive and courageous ex-boyfriend in high regard. (He made me describe him that way, but of course I would be lying if I said I didn't see him that way, too. And if he's reading this, thank you for those moments.)

Depression is like a cancer of the mind.

It just happens to some people, and the fight against it can sometimes kill you. People around you who begin to see your sickness become disgusted by you. They cannot understand what you feel, or why you feel it. They say to not dwell on the bad things, but don't they understand that you are not dwelling, but battling? Do they not understand that warfare must require participation? **My depression is fighting me, stabbing me, bleeding me dry, how can I just close my eyes and not feel that pain? Depression physically aches the body, not just the mind.**

When you are high functioning, people assume you are crying wolf when you say this. They assume you are desperate for attention. Maybe you are starved for attention, but that is additional, and the depression is not make-believe. I have a theory that extroverted people, not outgoing personalities but the people that truly draw energy from being around others, are more likely to suffer depression and are more likely to mask it well. We cannot be alone; we actually don't know how. I am a serial dater. The longest I spent being single was a period of eight months after I ruined what I am convinced of to this day was my one chance at true love and happiness ever after. I ruined it when my depression became out of control and I stopped masking it. I could only be around the people that didn't know me and didn't care to know me because the ones who cared for me asked questions I didn't want to answer and demanded me to be better than I wanted to be. I wanted to be pathetic for a while. **I was so tired of pretending I was adequate.** Those eight months were my penance, in a way, and were miserable. Now my average time spent being single is about a week.

I get a strange high from new relationships, but it comes with a lot of secret anxiety. I hate the beginning with someone when you are getting to know that person more intimately and go on fun dates. That part is usually the part people love the most, but not me. It makes me crazy. I just want to be comfortable with a person, and thus the weird high. It feels so good getting to know someone that I get too comfortable too fast, and so it ends prematurely and so I hate the beginning of relationships. I want to fast forward to the intimacy and the trust, things you can't fast forward to. That is when I truly feel safe and when my depression feels conquerable because I am not fighting alone.

I'll say it again because I think it is fitting and worth remembering: being depressed but high functioning is like clutching glass in both hands and pretending like you aren't

bleeding, like you then have to cook and clean with your gored palms. Your family is hungry and you must feed them. It is not crying wolf, and we are sorry it is too hard for you to hear about our sadness. We are sorry it is so draining for you to be the one we unload on all the time. **No sarcasm, I swear. We are truly sorry.** We need friendships, which means telling you the truth, finally, is the most liberating feeling in the world. It isn't the same to say it to a therapist, though that really does help, but to tell someone we love the truth about our sick brains and to be loved still, to be loved in spite of it, is healing. We are sorry, that as our friend we may require that cross for you to bear.

We would take it away if we could.

8

When The Sadness Returns Again (For No Real Reason At All)

Holly Riordan

Your alarm goes off, but you don't feel like getting out of bed. And after you pull on your clothes (all black) and finish your breakfast (just coffee), all you can think about is getting back *in* bed. The entire day, you're tired. Not physically. *Mentally.* And that's the worst kind of tired because sleep doesn't cure it. Even if you get a full eight hours, you still feel exhausted. Like you want to slip back into unconsciousness.

You're not looking forward to anything, even the things you're usually excited about. Once in a while, you'll actually manage a smile, a *genuine* smile over a TV show or a friend's joke, and in that moment you'll feel like you again. But the second the smile fades, you'll go right back to where you were at the start. Like nothing ever changed.

The worst part is that you feel like a complete asshole because you're always complaining. Always turning down invitations that require you to leave the house. Always forcing laughs when they should come genuinely. But you can't help it. If you could, then you wouldn't *choose* to be sad. You wouldn't *choose* to wake up every day, feeling useless. *Hopeless.*

You've been told, again and again, that it could be worse. So you think of all the great things in your life—and there *are* great things. You have parents that adore you and a pet that worships you and a warm bed to sleep in. But those thoughts don't make you feel any better. You just feel numb. And that numbness comes across as ungratefulness. As bitchiness. And you're worried that's how everyone else is starting to see you, as some ungrateful, depressed bitch.

You have an idea of what will push the sadness away—success, love, friends, a *purpose*. But you can't become successful when you're tethered to your bed all day. And you can't find love when you're too worn out to make small talk with strangers. The sadness causes more sadness. It traps you in a loop of unproductive pity.

Eventually, all of the sadness will fade away. And it'll stay away—maybe for a week. Maybe for five years. But you know that it's going to come back. You know that, no matter how much money you earn or how many countries you visit, you'll always be at its mercy. It'll sneak up on you and make you feel powerless again like you're unable to control your life, your destiny, *your own emotions.*

But you can't worry about tomorrow. You have to get through today. And *then* get through tomorrow. And tomorrow's tomorrow. Because you can't let the sadness win. It doesn't deserve a victory.

9

There Is A Huge Difference Between 'Being Sad' And Depression

Ari Eastman

Generally speaking, I'm not a very sad person. And maybe I've misrepresented myself with that. What with my endless melodrama and nauseating stories of *"I loved him, he didn't love me!"* people have started to categorize me as Sad Internet Girl. And I get it. You talk about depression, your dead dad, and unrequited love enough times, you'll get that title.

I recently did a few interviews about my poetry (OH HELLO—Shameless self-promotion, you can buy my collection here!) and the same theme kept coming up in questions: Ari is sad.

So let me clear this up: I'm, like, not sad? Is that weird? Should I continue to play this character crying into her wine glass every night and pining for past relationships? Because, this may shock you, but that isn't what I'm doing.

Okay, so maybe last Tuesday. But we won't count that.

I was first diagnosed with clinical depression when I was 14. I first found the vocabulary for it at 12, but it's hard to know if that was me or the raging war my body was fighting otherwise known as puberty. If someone could figure out a way to torture enemies by just making them relive puberty, it would be pretty brutal and useful. Though you'd have to deal with them slamming the door, blasting Avril Lavigne (or whatever the angsty preteens are listening to now—I'm out of touch at 23), and screaming into pillows. So, pick your battles, I guess.

My depression and anxiety went hand-in-hand, this weird little threesome that I really wasn't prepared for at the tender age of 14. It would be another two years before a boy kisses me on the mouth, but I was in a heavy-duty relationship with those two. My anxiety had me up all night, questioning things like mortality and the likelihood that the ceiling would suddenly cave and crush me into Pixie Stick dust. And then, like clockwork, my depression would show up for the party. "Babe! Have you been thinking about the universe exploding and eternal blackness? Oh FUN!!! This is my FAV part."

I was lucky to grow up with probably the two most understanding, empathetic parents known to mankind. I get that's a bold statement, but I really mean it. There was never shame in who I was or what I was feeling. My dad was a psychology professor and my mom had studied human development (but a writer at heart)—I basically had the parental jackpot for someone a little mentally abnormal.

As I started reaching my 20s, I noticed a pattern of manic episodes and depressive episodes. I hesitated in labeling anything because I was so sick of labels. People always want to make you something palatable. Here's the Funny Girl! Here's the Deep Artist! Here's the Virgin Mary! Here's the Madonna-Whore!—as if people can be categorized into something so singular.

I just started feeling so unbelievably over it. I had certain groups who solely identified me as the comedic relief. When things got uncomfortable, I made a joke. I was constantly trying to lighten the mood. I'd take shots at myself bringing self-deprecation to an art form. But I also had circles who knew me as a stand-in therapist. I was go-to for spilling secrets and sadness, and I would do my best to soak it up and offer my heart in return. I was living all these different versions of myself so sure they couldn't all exist at once.

And that's bullshit.

If someone tries to tell you to be one thing, it is, and always will be, bullshit. Look at your damn body! It's doing about a million things at once. So yeah, you are multifaceted too.

Having depression didn't cancel out my humor or ability to laugh. Sure, it made certain things harder and I had those Cymbalta commercial days of looking like a crumpled up napkin in bed—totally gross and used up. But it wasn't ALL I was. I wasn't just eternally Sad. I had depression. I have depression.

Being sad is an emotion. And emotions, by nature, are temporary creatures. I am sad when a relationship ends or I watch a video of a dog waiting by the grave of a soldier. And is sadness a side effect of depression? Well yeah, duh. Absolutely. But having depression and being sad are not exclusive beasts. Anyone can be sad. Everyone WILL be sad at some point. But not everyone has depression.

I don't know if I will ever vanquish depression fully. It is so much a part of my life and learning how to cope has in some ways made me a better person. I would still never wish it upon anyone else. Just like I'd never wish someone to have diabetes or heart disease or cancer. It's a disease. It has moments of remission and moments of ferocious activeness. But I'm not just Sad Internet Girl.

I won't ever hide my depression or pretend she doesn't exist inside me. I have times I don't know how to separate my depression from the rest of me. And I know that's okay. But never forget, if you have depression, there is no reason you won't have days of laughing and smiling. You aren't destined to a lifetime of "sad" because of this. You might have to practice a bit more self-care, listen and check in with your body, push against things those around you don't understand, but you aren't cursed to just be Sad Girl or Sad Boy or Sad Them.

I have depression, and today? I am not sad. I am at a coffee shop smiling at a cute boy across from me. The lilacs outside are thriving and I'm listening to "Surf" by Donnie Trumpet & The Social Experiment. Today, I feel light and full of possibility.

I have depression, and today? I am happy.

10

It's Not Always Easy To Be Happy, And That's Okay

Tatiana Pérez

Sometimes, it's hard to be happy.

I've realized that happiness is weird. Like, conceptually. That it's something we expect from people—that is, we expect people to be happy. And that when people are unhappy, we assume they're doing something wrong.

I realize I'm not the first person to come to this realization.

Unhappy with your job? Work harder. Get a promotion. Or stop whining, quit, and start a new career. Unhappy with your partner? See a couple's therapist. Make it work. Or get your shit together and break up, because no one wants to *hear it.* K?

"If you make good choices and avoid major fuck ups, your life will be good," we tell each other. "You'll be happy."

Most people want to be happy by most conventional metrics

of happiness (good health, love, money). Most people want to see the best in most situations so they can be happy. In other words, most people try to will their happiness into being.

To be clear, I am most people.

I've been told I'm an optimist. I don't think that's always meant as a compliment. I think my optimism often presents itself as blind. As bullshit. As not taking into account the sad reality of the present situation. I think that's true. Optimism is hopefulness. And hopefulness is predicated on some ignorance of the worst possible outcomes of, again, the present situation.

Over the past two years or so, I've experienced some extended bouts of severe unhappiness. Through those depressive periods, in the moments I've seen clearly, I've tried to tweak the tweakable materials of my depression. Live consciously. Quit Adderall. Talk to my family more often. Be a more available friend.

There are times, though, when I feel like there's nothing I can do to improve my condition. That I'm bound to be unhappy. That I'll inevitably mirror sources of my unhappiness. That my emotional fate is out of my control. That I can be a good person, but that my life won't match my character. That the world is, actually, not that good.

My depression says, "My world is deeply flawed. It won't let me be happy."

When my consciousness takes one of those turns, I know that people like me less. Because when I'm unhappy, it's a little bit harder for people around me to be happy. Not just because I'm "moody"—moods (especially when they're not yours) are incredibly annoying—but because depression stands against the cultural imperative to be happy.

Funnily enough, I'm writing about unhappiness, finally, because right now, I do feel happy. I've felt mostly happy for a few weeks. And I guess it's fair to say that I've been choosing happiness. I haven't been taking Adderall. I've been calling my parents. Both good choices I intend to keep making. But the process has been a little more complex than simply "choosing happiness" allows.

I don't want to disempower myself in this whole business of happiness. You heard it here first: I'm trying to be happy. I want to make good choices, and I want to be happy.

But sometimes, yes, it's hard.

11

I Promise I'll Stop Saying 'I'm Okay' When I'm Not (And Other Lies I Tell Myself)

Becca Martin

It's turning into an everyday routine. I wake up and tell myself it will be a good day. But it rarely is. I'm stuck alone all day with my thoughts and they just progressively get worse as the hours pass and the day turns to night.

I try to convince myself when I'm alone with my thoughts to think positively, but it never works. I'm stuck alone with my feelings and I can't escape them.

The silence grows greater with every passing tick on the clock and I have nowhere to run; the feelings are just dancing around in my head and I can't escape them.

I can't do anything but accept them, let them continue to dance while all I can do is sit here and let them because I'm too tired to fight them off anymore.

Lately, I've been trying to laugh but it's been getting harder. It's been getting lost behind the voices in my own head telling me this isn't where I belong. It's been getting lost behind my own personal hell I've been trying to fight, a battle I'm constantly losing.

I know it's become apparent in my eyes, that they can blatantly tell you that I'm not okay, **but most people still just look away.**

In a way, I don't want you to notice because I don't want to drown you in my problems and become a burden. But part of me is screaming for someone to actually ask me what's wrong and want to hear the answer.

Part of me is begging to be saved, part of me is begging for someone to care enough to ask me if I'm okay and actually wait to hear the answer.

I don't know how much longer I can cry for help silently right in front of you.

I tell myself that next time someone asks me what's wrong, I won't say I'm okay, I'll actually tell them, but the words won't come out of my mouth.

What I really want to tell you, what I really want to get off my chest won't come out.

The only thing that comes out with "I'm okay" is tears because when my mouth doesn't explain the way I feel my eyes express themselves.

It just adds to the list of promises I make to myself. I promise myself I will stop pretending everything is okay when it clearly isn't. I promise myself that if I just stay a little longer everything will work out. I promise myself that tomorrow I'll have a different mindset. I promise myself that when I wake up in the morning that the world won't be as miserable.

I promise myself a lot of things, but the one thing I always fail to keep my promise about is admitting I'm not okay because I want to think of myself as stronger.

It's a desperate cry for help, while at the same time keeping it locked up inside. It's a never-ending cycle of self-torture that I just can't stop.

It's the constant self-inflicting pain that I can't get enough of.

I'll sit with my own pain, I'll let the voices dance in my head while I can't escape my own thoughts and I'll continue to tell myself that I'm okay.

I'm not as okay as I pretend to be, but maybe one day I will be.

12

11 Things People Don't Realize You Are Doing Because Of Your Depression

Lauren Jarvis-Gibson

1. You do everything you can to try to hide the fact that you have it.

When you have depression, you try to convince yourself that you are completely fine. You put on a fake smile wherever you go and your friends envy your enthusiasm and energy that you always seem to have. But inside? You feel drained, lost and terribly sad.

2. You lash out at loved ones.

You tend to lose your temper over things other people wouldn't even get worked up about. You harbor a lot of negative energy inside of your heart and sometimes lashing out is the only thing that you can do to get it all out.

3. You redo everything.

Whether it's a school paper or an Excel sheet for work, you redo it over and over again until your eyes are glazed over. You are a complete perfectionist and you can't stop trying to please everybody else around you.

4. You self-medicate.

You can't just have one glass of wine at dinner if you are feeling terribly depressed. Alcohol is a depressant, but it makes you forget about your problems for a little bit. You know this is incredibly unhealthy for you to do, but you can't help but want to get away from your problems for a night.

5. You cancel plans that you actually want to go to.

Whether it be that wedding you've been dying to go to, or that great concert your friends can't stop raving about, sometimes you won't be able to handle it and you will cancel. This doesn't mean you wanted to cancel, but in your mental state, sometimes you need to be alone.

6. You ache everywhere.

Depression, just like anxiety, can also cause physical symptoms. Sometimes this mental illness can cause your body to feel like it weighs a ton, and every bone in your body will hurt.

7. You can't stay awake.

Insomnia is a huge part of mental illnesses, and depression can definitely cause you to have sleeping problems. It also can be hard to stay awake during the day because you have no motivation whatsoever and feel too fatigued to do anything.

8. You eat everything in sight.

Depression can cause you to want to eat 'your feelings.' When you aren't feeling good mentally, food can be the only thing that can provide you with comfort when you feel most alone.

9. You lose your appetite.

The opposite can also happen and you could lose the majority of your appetite. With depression, comes a great loss of energy and enthusiasm for participating in activities. Eating may be one of those things.

10. You make your life look perfect on the outside.

You don't want anyone to worry about you, so you try your hardest to tell your friends you are fine. You do your best to post smiling and cute pictures on your social media channels and you do whatever it takes to not have to be asked, 'are you depressed?'

11. You cry for no reason.

Sometimes, you wake up with tears rolling down your face. Some days, you could be happy in an instant and then start to weep the very next second. You constantly think to yourself 'Why am I sad? Why am I crying? I should be happy.' **But, depression is an illness. It can't be fixed with a cast or a Band-Aid. It is truly a chemical imbalance in the brain, and it is not your fault. It is never your fault.**

13

Please Don't Say You're 'Dealing' With My Depression

Sara Huggins

This is a message for anyone who has ever had any kind of interaction with someone who suffers from a mental illness—so, every single one of you. Here are some things that I wish everyone knew about the way we talk about mental illness and those who have them. Please keep in mind that you may know someone without knowing their story, so regardless of who you are talking to, please keep these things in mind.

First of all, the language that we use when talking about mental illness can sometimes be harmful without us realizing it. Something that really gets me is when people say they have to "deal with me." The problem with this word is that it makes being helped sound like some kind of burden. The word *dealing* implies an almost instant sense of negativity. It absolutely irks me and makes me want to scream. When someone uses this term with me, I almost immediately feel like a burden to them.

Feeling like a burden is a really big problem for me personally, as well as many people I know who suffer from mental illness.

It is always accompanied by a huge amount of guilt, whether we truly are a burden or not. By you using this word, you are telling us that we are indeed burdening you, which is something that we already feared and you have just confirmed.

So this brings me to:

What words could we use instead?

One saying that I like to use with is "working with." As soon as you say it, it sounds like you are now a team, united for a similar outcome. Both parties are willing to put work in and work towards a goal. That person who needs you is no longer standing alone—they have an ally. Having someone by your side makes everything seem easier since you are no longer doing it alone. For example, you could say, "I am working with Sara to help with her depression" as opposed to "I have been dealing with Sara and her depression." Sounds better, doesn't it?

Replacing the word *dealing* with the word *helping* is also good. Everyone needs help sometimes, and so to use a word that we use every day in all kinds of situations, it seems to help remove some of the stigma of the burden of mental illness. The word *helping* can be used in the place of *dealing with* in almost every possible situation so the switch should be easy!

All of this is just a reminder, to please choose your words wisely and keep in mind that you never really know who might be suffering internally. If you are unsure of what may or may not be acceptable ways to approach or talk about mental health, asking someone what they feel comfortable with is always a good plan. Everyone interprets things differently and may or may not be hurt by some of the things that I am. Just keep in mind that the power of positivity is immense and that the kinder you speak to others, the kinder they will speak to themselves.

14

What It's Like To Be The Child Of Someone With Depression

Ella Ceron

It seems so self-serving to play that game. You know the one. **"Where were you when you heard…?"** Yet here we are. Playing it. Again.

We live in an ever-connected world. We have instantaneous access to global events, world-changing tragedies, and even the little things that we make matter. Who married whom, who had a baby and what "unique" name they gave that child, who died. I remember where I was when I heard that Whitney Houston died—getting out of the subway at 57th and 7th—when Cory Monteith died, and now. Now with Robin Williams' passing, it's not about drug use (though that was something Williams was never shy about admitting he needed help with) but rather something that much more pervasive, that much more common, that much more taboo for all its pedestrian ways. Depression.

And so, when I heard that Robin Williams had presumably taken his own life, that he had been fighting a tremendous battle with depression, I sat on the floor of my bedroom and cried. I cried, and I texted friends; and I watched *The Birdcage*, which was the first movie to ever really sink it into my head that there is something so wonderful about loving yourself and who you are and how you want to express yourself in every way that you want to do it; and I cried as I watched that movie; and I called my mom, and we got into a fight, which is dumb to say but it's true.

I called to tell her that I love her, and I spent the next hour with her on the phone, in tears because—selfishly, honestly—it is my biggest fear that I will wake up one day and hear, on a much smaller scale than Williams' news, that my mother has taken her life.

My mother has been battling chronic depression since before I was born. She has been on more medications than even she can remember, and she's seen more doctors and therapists and psychologists and social workers than anyone else I know. And I'm from Los Angeles, where *dogs* have therapists. (We always make this joke because we have to because we need to laugh about it, because there is no other way.)

I remember all the days when she wouldn't get out of bed. All the days when she'd go back to take a nap on a Saturday and spend the next five hours in the kind of sleep that is almost deathlike itself. I remember all the times she'd burst out into tears when we had minor disagreements, all the times she thought that my saying no, I didn't want to do something was a direct rejection of not just the idea, but of her person. All the times she blamed me for her mood. All the times she forgot to take her pills that morning and I was left with someone spiraling in public, someone who needed to be coached to get home.

I remember when I was 15 and only had a learner's permit, and had to go to the library so I could write a paper, but she was in one of her moods and told me to just take the car myself. (The driving age in California is 16.) Even though I had never driven on the freeway by myself. Even though I could not legally drive myself. I had to have my paper done the next day.

I remember when she admitted to me that sometimes, she would take a bath and wonder what it would be like to just. You know.

That's not something you can ever forget, really.

Often, it would be the sound of my voice, or of my brother's voice, or the cat, maybe, that would snap her out of these moments. But to know that it's something your parent is thinking about is terrifying. I often wonder if I made the right choice in moving 3,000 miles away. What if something happens and I can't get back in time?

You never really know, do you? That even the funniest people — the most gregarious, the most loving, the most engaging and charismatic and wonderful and kindest — have their demons. We all have the things that haunt us. And we all have the things that overpower us from time to time.

A lot of people are making news of the fact that Williams' last offering to the social world was an Instagram photo of him with his daughter, Zelda, when she was young. She's 25 and has therefore known only a father who had already acknowledged and sought help for his demons. Having depression doesn't make you any less wonderful a parent. It doesn't make you any less loving or (for the most part) capable of taking care of this smaller creature who is made of your genes. Sometimes you need a little help, whether that's medication or therapy or exercise or anything else. But I'd imagine the world he created for Zelda and her brothers was wonderful and full of love and light and laughter, whatever storm was brewing inside him at any given moment. (That's how it worked with my mother, too; she is a woman from whom I'd be lucky to say I inherited my sense of humor.)

To be the child of someone with depression is to be born into a world where you know you are predisposed to a certain level of sadness. It's inevitable. It's a chemical thing, and much like cancer or hair color, they sometimes pass it along. There's a certain amount of nurture at play, too, and if you grow up in a house that is very good at being sad, chances are you will be good at being sad, too. And there is *such* a burden. A duty. A responsibility. *I have to be a good kid today because Mom already has enough on her plate. Because Dad is sick and can't help himself. Because if they love me, maybe they'll be happy.*

They can love you, and still be unhappy.

But maybe, if you tell them you love them—hopefully, you can only ever hope—they'll feel a little less alone. A little less drowned in their own dark shadows, all those craggy parts of the mind that they think nobody else cares to help them fix. But people do care, and people will listen, and people will understand. We all have a certain level of sadness in ourselves. But what we also have is love.

Losing Robin Williams is, to many people who grew up with his movies, like losing a member of the family. Someone whom you loved so much and figured would always be there. I can only imagine what it's like to lose your actual father, and I hope I won't have to learn how to cope with that anytime soon. The same thing goes with losing my mother. Especially to something like depression.

Sometimes people with depression never manage to find or even ask for help, and it's up to those who love them to check in. But we live in a world that places such a premium on the opposite of depression—on that ever-elusive dream of *happy*, whatever that is—that sometimes we forget that sometimes all we need is just to be okay. Knowing that someone is there. That they will listen. That they care.

That there is more to live for, that there are things to be happy about, that there is a life outside of the darkness. That all you need is to *try* to get through to the next morning, the next hour. We're only ever given one life. And all we can do is try to give as much love as we can, to everyone who knows us. Robin Williams did that. Here's hoping he's finally found his happiness, too.

15

8 Things Your Girlfriend With Depression Wants You To Know

Ari Eastman

1. Your love won't cure her.

I think this comes from a good place, really, I do. When we love someone, we want to take away all their pain. We never want to see them suffering. It's a natural response, a nurturing desire to help the people we care about. But you need to remember your love is not a medication.

2. She's not broken.

This is such a damaging stereotype we assign to people with depression—that they are 'broken' people who need fixing. No. She has an illness that she didn't ask for. No one does.

3. It's not just in her head.

And yes, I get the irony in that sentence. But this isn't something she just made up or imagined. It's very real and affects her life in ways you'll probably never even realize.

4. And no, she can't positively think it away.

You wouldn't encourage someone with cancer or diabetes to just think better thoughts, would you? This kind of mentality is dangerous and one that stops people from actively getting the real help they need. Instead, encourage her to talk to her medical or mental health professionals to figure out the best route to take.

5. She's afraid of being perceived as a burden.

You might notice that she doesn't readily open up or (especially if the relationship is new) tries to hide her symptoms. Because depression can be so consuming, it's not uncommon for feelings of guilt to accompany it. She never wants you to feel like this is something you got stuck with. So as a result, she might withhold certain things.

6. It hurts. Physically.

Research has shown that people suffering from depression have three times the average risk of developing chronic pain.

7. She doesn't expect you to fully understand.

It's impossible to put ourselves in someone else's shoes if we haven't been there. We can try all we want, but that's all it ever will be. *Trying.* She knows that. She's not anticipating you're going to always get it. But she does want you to validate what she experiences. Saying something like, "Though I might not know how this feels, I support you and am here for you," can go a long way.

8. The way she feels about you is totally separate from her illness.

It can be hard loving someone with depression. Hard for both people. And one thing she never wants you to think is that because she struggles, it somehow means she isn't happy to be with you. Just because this is something she deals with, she can still love you with her entire heart. She never wants you to question that.

16

What It's Like To Be In Love When You Have Depression

Holly Everett

"No one will love you until you learn to love yourself" is an easy enough phrase to believe is true. But it's terrifying, especially when you have depression. What if you never learn? As a teenager, it made me fear for my life as an adult. I was certain I would never be capable of being in a relationship, but I was very wrong. Honestly, I do not like myself very much, and in August of 2013, a boy fell very, very much in love with me.

I have dealt with depression for as long as I can remember. I've been on and off medications, been to therapy, but it's still alive and well, comfortable in its home in my bones. I can feel it every day, a tiny inkling that causes breathtaking emotional pain at the most inconvenient of times.

My depression doesn't care that I am in a relationship with a boy who makes me laugh, tells me I'm beautiful 20 times a day, and cares more deeply for me than any other boy has. I am grateful for the nights he holds me while I cry for hours for no reason. I am thankful that he puts up with my random periods of irritability. He constantly attempts to comfort me if I am suddenly uncomfortable when we're out in public. He fills me with hope for the future when I lead myself down the darkest of paths, plays with my hair when I'm having trouble sleeping, and encourages me to eat when I have no appetite. He takes care of me and I never even had to explain myself. I still consciously think to myself, nine months into this relationship, "Wow, someone is in love with me." I often think about how lucky I am to be loved, regardless of my flaws in chemistry.

This intense love is frightening because every day, I fear that one more thing will push him over the edge. That one more time of me rolling over in bed, teary-eyed, for no reason, could push him away. I know it upsets him, and I reassure him through my salty, blurred vision that it's not his fault. I am often overcome with guilt and I hate that my feelings about myself cause any pain on his part. Sometimes he is not easily convinced, but I try as hard as I can with the little energy I have. Some of our nights end in a tight hug and an "I'm sorry" mumbled from my lips, but I'm just thankful that he is still happy to wake up to me every morning.

Every day is a struggle. I am constantly on edge, going back and forth between caring too much and not caring at all, wondering when he will have enough. He is quick to remind me how much he loves me, but I am just as quick to be overcome with crippling doubt. We both know that this is how forever will be, and if he hasn't given up yet, I'm certain that he is 100% all in.

Never let anyone tell you that you are not worth being loved if you don't love yourself. Never let anyone tell you that your mental illness is the reason why you are not in a relationship. Never let anyone tell you that you should smile more, fix your hair, or wear more color. Never let anyone makes you feel bad about what you can't always control.

Someone will be in love with you regardless of your most comfortable state, and if that happens to be curled up on the floor of your room, crying as you listen to your favorite sad songs, then you have found true love.

17

13 Things To Remember When You Love A Person Who Has Depression

Koty Neelis

1. Depression is *not* a choice.

Depression is one of the most helpless and frustrating experiences a person can have. It's sometimes feeling sad, sometimes feeling empty, and sometimes feeling absolutely nothing at all. There are times when depression can leave someone feeling paralyzed in their own mind and body, unable to do the things they used to love to do or the things they know they should be doing. Depression is not just a bad day or a bad mood and it's not something someone can just "get over." Remember no one chooses to be depressed.

2. Saying things like "it'll get better," "you just need to get out of the house," or "you'll be fine" is meaningless.

It's easy to tell someone these things because you think you're giving them a solution or a simple way to make them feel better and to ease their pain, but these kinds of phrases always come across as empty, insulting, and essentially meaningless.

Saying these phrases to them only create more tension within, making them feel as though they're inadequate, and like you're not acknowledging what they're going through by trying to put a Band-Aid on a much larger issue. They understand you're just trying to help but these words only make them feel worse. A silent hug can do so much more than using cliched sayings.

What you can say instead:

I'm here for you. I believe in you. I believe you are stronger than this and I believe you'll get through this. What can I do to help you? What do you think would make you feel better?

Avoid offering advice but instead just let them know you're there for them and ask them questions to help guide them in discovering what could make them feel better.

3. Sometimes they have to push you away before they can bring you closer.

People who suffer from depression often get frustrated with

feeling like they're a burden on other people. This causes them to isolate themselves and push away people they need the most, mentally exhausting themselves from worrying about if they're weighing their loved ones down with their sadness. If they become distant, just remember to let them know you're still there, but don't try to force them to hang out or talk about what's going on if they don't want to.

4. You're allowed to get frustrated.

Just because someone deals with depression doesn't mean you have to cater to all of their needs or walk on eggshells when you're around them. Depressed people need to feel loved and supported but if it begins to create a negative impact on your life you're allowed to acknowledge this and figure out how to show them love and kindness without self-sacrificing.

5. It's important to discuss and create boundaries.

In those moments of frustration it's important to take a step back and look at how you can help the depressed person while also maintaining your own sense of happiness and fulfillment. Be patient. Talk to them about your concerns and explain the boundaries you need to create within your relationship. Find out something that works for both of you.

6. They can become easily overwhelmed.

Constant exhaustion is a common side effect of depression.

Just getting through the day can be an overwhelming and exhausting experience. They may seem and look totally fine one moment and in the next moment feel tired and have no energy at all, even if they're getting plenty of sleep every night. This can result in them canceling plans suddenly, leaving events early, or saying no to things altogether. Just remember it's not about anything you did. It's just one of the prevalent side effects of living with the disease.

7. It's not about you.

When you have a loved one dealing with depression it can be difficult to understand what they're going through and to consider how their sadness is a reflection of your relationship with them. If they need space or become distant don't blame yourself and wonder how you could do things differently to heal them. Understand their depression is not about you.

8. Avoid creating ultimatums, making demands, or using a "tough-love" approach.

Telling someone you're going to break up with them or not talk to them anymore if they don't get better is not going to magically cure them of their illness. They won't suddenly become the person you want them to be just because you're tired of dealing with their problems. It's a personal decision to walk away from someone if their issues become too much for you and your relationship with them, but thinking the 'tough-love' approach will make them better is unrealistic and manipulative.

9. They don't always want to do this alone.

Many often assume people dealing with depression want to just be left alone. While there are may be times when they want their space, this doesn't mean they want to face their fears completely alone. Offer to take them on a drive somewhere. Ask if they want to get coffee or a meal. One on one time where you can bring them out of their routine and where you two can connect can often mean everything for them. Reach out to them unexpectedly. Remind them they don't have to do this alone.

10. Try not to compare your experiences with theirs.

When someone is going through a rough time we often want to share with them our own stories to let them know you've gone through something similar and can relate to their struggle. When you say something like, "Oh yeah, this one time I was depressed too…" it only makes them feel like you're minimizing their pain. Express empathy but don't suppress their feelings. The greatest resource you can share with your friend is your ability to listen. That's all they really need.

11. It's okay to ask your friend where they are in their feelings.

How are they really feeling and how are they coping with their depression? Suicidal thoughts are a common occurrence for depressed people and it's okay to directly ask them ways they're practicing self-care and to come up with a safety plan for times when their depression becomes too overwhelming.

12. Schedule time to spend together.

Offer to spend time with them once or twice a week to exercise, grocery shop, or hang out together. Ask if you can cook dinner with them and plan a friend date. One of the hardest parts of depression is feeling too exhausted to cook healthy meals, so you can really help them out by cooking food they can store in their fridge or freezer for a later time.

13. Just because someone is depressed doesn't mean that they're weak.

In his book *Against Happiness: In Praise Of Melancholia*, author Eric G. Wilson explores the depths of sadness and how experiencing mental anguish can actually make us more empathetic, creative people. Although he explains the difference between depression and melancholia, he rejects the idea of inflated happiness our culture and society is obsessed with, and instead explains why we reap benefits from the darker moments in life. Wilson writes:

> *"I for one am afraid that our American culture's overemphasis on happiness at the expense of sadness might be dangerous, a wanton forgetting of an essential part of a full life. I further am wary in the face of this possibility: to*

desire only happiness in a world undoubtedly tragic is to become inauthentic, to settle for unrealistic abstractions that ignore concrete situations. I am finally fearful over our society's efforts to expunge melancholia from the system. Without the agitations of the soul, would all of our magnificently yearning towers topple? Would our heart-torn symphonies cease?"

In a similar manner psychiatrist and philosopher, Dr. Neel Burton, discusses in his TEDx talk about how some of the most influential and important people in history have experienced depression. He explains the way our culture looks at and treats depression and how traditional societies differ in their approach, seeing human distress as an indicator of the need to address important life problems, not a mental illness.

It's important to remember depression is not something that should be considered shameful and experiencing it doesn't make someone weak or inadequate.

18

What It's Like To Love Someone Who Has Depression

Heidi Priebe

When you love someone who has depression, you're going to think that it's your fault. No matter how many people tell you otherwise, no matter how educated you are on the topic, and no matter what you logically know to be true, your heart is going to draw its own conclusions. *You weren't attentive enough, it will tell you. You traveled too often. You called too sparsely. You didn't see the warning signs that you should have seen.* You'll grow accustomed to an anvil of guilt that nestles into the pit of your stomach. *You could have prevented this,* will be your mantra. It won't be true, but it will be there.

When you love someone who has depression, you'll over-correct. You'll want to make up for every day you were not there with 12 days where you are. You'll bring over cookies and funny movies. You'll be attentive and present. You'll read books about supporting someone with depression and you'll become a textbook version of the perfect companion. You'll listen instead of speak. You'll support instead of judge. You'll say the words "I understand" more times than you can count. You will promise to weather out the storm with them. You'll mean it.

When you love someone who has depression, you will think that you can fix it. You'll become a walking inventory of all the different tactics they could try. "Why not antidepressants?" you will ask them. "Why not therapy? Or exercise? Exercise helps in up to 80% of cases of depression, did you know that?" You will get accustomed to being shut down. You will not mind. You'll go about it with the relentless enthusiasm of a high school cheerleader—fiercely believing that something will get through to them soon. It just has to. You know it.

When you love someone who has depression, you will become frustrated. *They're just not trying hard enough,* you'll decide. *They could get over this.* Your brain will be locked in a constant battle with itself, one-half rational and unwavering, the other emotional and frazzled. You will swing between feelings of outward anger and inward guilt with lightning speed. You won't be able to work out whose fault all this is; only that it's *someone's.* Because it has to be. Because if not then who's ever going to fix it?

When you love someone who has depression, you will miss them. You will watch the person you once shared so many joys with shrink hopelessly into themselves. One day you'll think back to the happier times you shared and feel struck by the contrast of how things are now. You'll get the distinct feeling that someone you love has passed away. You will mourn that person. You'll sift through old pictures and love letters and cry. You'll realize you may never get that same person back and you'll feel sorry: not just for them but also for yourself. For the happier times that are over now. The times that you aren't sure you will ever get back.

When you love someone who has depression, you will think about giving up. The image you once had of your ability to overcome any situation become punctured: Shot to the heart by a single, unforgiving diagnosis. You cannot fix this. You cannot save them. This understanding will warp your understanding of the world so badly that you will start to feel helpless yourself. Start to sense that dragging undercurrent of despair twisting itself around your ankles. You will want to entertain it, but you won't. Because when you love someone who has depression, you will never give up. You will not step down. You will support and love and hope and endure for as long as it damn well takes. There will not be another choice. There never has been.

When you love someone who has depression, you will simply keep on loving. Because in the end, you will know that it's all you can do.

19

7 Beautiful Ways Loving Someone With Depression Changed Me

Kristen Lem

"It's not going to be easy," he warned me. He was right. But it wasn't the hardest thing. Walking away was. Our story didn't end well, but that's OK. I'm a better person for it, and here's why:

I stopped labeling people.

Depression is just one aspect of someone's personality. I have a tendency to group people, stereotype even; not because I'm prejudice, but because I'm efficient. This works well for office supplies, herbs, and spices. Not human beings. We are multi-faceted and it was only when I loved someone so complex that I could appreciate this.

Unforgettable moments.

Have you ever experienced something that you just know will never happen again? Once my friend and I found ourselves in a hot tub full of professional tennis players. It's sort of like that. Loving a depressed person is characterized with the highest highs and the lowest lows. There were feelings and moments so silly, sweet, and profound that I know I'll never have again.

My heart opened in ways I never knew existed.

The worst part about a depressed person is not their depression. It's actually the glimpses of their smile. Their laugh, sweetness, and vulnerability. That hurts the most because you know it exists. The ability to be happy is there somewhere and you'd do anything to make it last. Call it co-dependency, but before this, I wasn't willing to sacrifice much. Now that it's all over, it's as if my heart expanded during the relationship, now with more capacity to love again.

I became a better friend.

"I …like…don't even understand why she's with him." We've all said that. Heard that. Your good friends will say it to your face after he disappoints you again and again. You'll make excuses and stick up for him. But when it's all over, you won't be so quick to judge when it happens to someone else. That disapproving look turns into a nod and "yeah … I know. Sucks. I'm sorry."

No small talk.

People who ponder the dark side understand life's complexities and see all the horrible things that go on in their heads and in the world. As a result, these people are deep, sensitive, and usually have interesting things to say. Questions like, "How was your day?" are awful because their day was probably shitty. And if that's the case, they definitely don't want to know how yours was.

I learned to take the good with the bad.

If you've ever spent any length of time with a depressed person, you know he or she is not depressed all the time. In fact, your boyfriend or girlfriend is probably really funny and pleasant sometimes. After a few erratic mood swings, I stopped anticipating a "bad day" and just enjoyed the good times when we had them. It was a practice of "being in the moment," something we could probably all use more of.

My boundaries became clear.

When I made the decision to end things, it wasn't because of depression. I would've stuck by him if he was willing to stick by me. It's easy to be in love when things are peachy. Can you still have love during the bad times? Walking away I knew I could. For someone else.

20

This Is How To Be Friends With Someone Who's Struggling

Alexandria Brown

It's pain. You feel it in your heart looking at your loved one who's struggling. You want to do anything to help them. You want to tell them how wonderful they are. You want to explain how much love you have for them. You're not sure they'd hear it right now, though.

Actually, you're definitely sure they won't.

You see them day in and day out fighting the intangible demons in their soul and you just want to fight with them. You want to stand at their side and tell them that you know how strong they are. That this is something that's temporary and this too shall pass. You've seen them come back from darker moments but you're not sure if this is the one that breaks the camel's back. If they're too far gone for them to snap themselves out of their depression.

You want to be their strength in this time of weakness. You want to carry them on your back as their knees get weaker and weaker and standing becomes almost too much for them to bear. As life kicks them square in the jaw, you're the one picking them up every time and reminding them that they can do this. **They can get through this.**

How do I know about the pain you're feeling while struggling to love your loved one? I see that same pain in the faces of the people who love me every time I feel like giving up. I hear the determination in their voice to try to save me when I'm at my lowest point in my depression.

I feel their love when the numbness takes over my entire body and getting out of bed isn't going to happen that day.

I fully believe people with mental illnesses are warriors who are so strong embracing their struggles and dealing with their shit. I also know that they're loved ones, our loved ones, are heroes. Sometimes our loved ones are the only shining beacon of light in such a dark and painful times.

I know for myself it's hard for me to appreciate those people when I'm struggling. It's hard for me to remember every single person who showers me with unconditional love when my heart is broken into millions of little pieces. Those people though crouch beside me and help me pick up the pieces time and time again. They lay next to me when I can't get out of bed and comfort me by just being there.

I know there are things you wish you could do. A way to take the pain away that's plaguing your loved one so bad right now. I know that there's a need to fix everything. I also know that there's a helplessness you feel when you realize that sometimes you can't do something specifically to help.

Sometimes there isn't a right thing to say. Sometimes there isn't a right thing to do. No matter what the love that you give is enough. It's enough to be just a phone call away. It's enough to just give us a hug when things feel like they're collapsing. **It's enough to just be there.**

So this is an appreciation to all the loved ones out there loving the shit out of people who have mental illnesses. This is also for the people who don't turn their back when someone is struggling to deal with their heartache. This is for the people who manage to continuously love no matter what.

You are appreciated for being you and for loving us when we need it most. Thank you.

21

50 One-Sentence Reminders For Anyone Who Is Having 'One Of Those Days'

Kendra Syrdal

1. It's just a bad day, not a bad life.

2. Feeling sad or down in the dumps doesn't make you pathetic, it means you're a human.

3. Some great art came because of great sadness.

4. Depression is out of your control, not doing anything BECAUSE of it is well within your control.

5. Somewhere out there, someone is probably smiling because of you.

6. If you have a roof over your head and food in your fridge, you're already doing better than a lot of people.

7. "I just don't feel like it," is a perfectly acceptable reason to pass on something.

8. Being kind to yourself is never, ever selfish.

9. You can get out of bed because if you find it's too much, you can always get back in.

10. There is an expiration date on how long you will feel sad.

11. Tomorrow is another day.

12. Everything is temporary.

13. Finding your own strength is one of the strongest things you can possibly do.

14. Being self-reliant is an amazing feat that you should be proud of.

15. But asking for help is equally as admirable.

16. Sometimes you won't know why you're in a mood, and that's okay.

17. If someone doesn't 'get' bad moods, they're just completely in their own world and you don't need to pay attention to them.

18. There are so many people who deal with depression every day; you are not alone.

19. You don't have to run a marathon, you can just go to the store.

20. It's the little things that count.

21. "You is kind, you is smart, you is important."

22. It takes a certain amount of maturity to be able to say, "I'm in a bad mood but I will keep going anyway."

23. When you feel your pulse beating, it means you've survived everything and you're still here.

24. There is no shame in saying, "I can't do this alone."

25. But there is also no shame in needing to deal with it by yourself if that's what feels right.

26. It is totally okay and valid to be sad for no reason (or for a stupid reason).

27. But admitting this is what takes the power away from the sadness.

28. Being in touch with your emotions means you're self-aware, so congratulations.

29. There is no right way or wrong way to take care of yourself.

30. Sometimes even just drinking water, going outside, or even stretching can make all of the difference.

31. But sometimes it won't—and you aren't a failure if it doesn't.

32. Take care of yourself, others second.

33. It's okay (and even helpful) to laugh at yourself and your moods.

34. Even Obama has bad days.

35. If all you did today was shower, you're still doing better than a lot of people.

36. "If Britney can make it through 2007, you can make it through today."

37. Your pain is an excuse to be in a bad mood, but not an excuse to be cruel.

38. Apologize when you need to not only to other people, but also to yourself.

39. You are not selfish for saying, "I can only take care of me right now."

40. If something is making you feel worse, it's okay to remove it from your life.

41. If Zoloft helps you, that's awesome.

42. But if just going for walk does the trick, that's awesome too.

43. Sometimes just acknowledging what's bringing you down is enough to take the power away from it.

44. You will not be miserable forever.

45. It's okay (actually more than okay, it's empowering) to be able to laugh through your pain.

46. Sleeping it off is just as valid for sadness as it is for hangovers.

47. It's okay to feel like a roller coaster—you're normal.

48. Crying about nothing is still a perfectly acceptable reason to cry.

49. Mental health and self-care are things that you have to work on forever.

50. So take it one day at a time.

22

Here's What I'm Going To Tell You Instead Of 'It Will Get Better'

Rania Naim

When you're going through a hard time, it's easy for people to tell you things like *it will get better* or *'it will be okay,* they don't understand that these words; even though they're true, they don't really help and they don't ease the pain. Sometimes they can add to the frustration because it simply doesn't tell you what you want to hear. That's not what you want to hear when you're suffering. You don't want to hear what you already know. So instead of telling you it's going to get better, here's what I'll tell you:

I understand your pain.

Either because I've been there before or because I know what it's like to be profoundly sad, to feel like there is no one in the world who will understand you, to feel like you're the only one struggling, to feel like there's just no point in living anymore. I'll tell you that I understand you, that you are not alone and that I know what you're going through so you don't have to waste your time explaining it to me. *I get it.*

I have faith in you.

I have faith in your strength, in your ability to rise back up after the fall, in your persistence to fight through the worst days of your life and in your courage to start over. I have faith that you will find your way out of the darkness and slowly let the light back in. I have faith that you will heal yourself because you can; *because you will.*

I trust you.

I really do. I know you will not destroy yourself, I know you will come to realize that certain things happen for you to grow, for you to believe, for you to *change* and for you to grow wiser. I trust that you will understand the lessons life is trying to teach you, that you will discover the beauty within you when you're hurting and I trust that you will become more compassionate, kinder and ready to dedicate your life to helping others come out of their darkness too.

I'm not worried about you.

I'm not scared that you will fall into severe depression or stay in the dark, I'm not concerned that you will never smile again. I know you will, when the time is right, *you will.* I know you will smile again and laugh again and breathe again. I know you will shine brighter than before and I know you will have a different outlook on life, a better perspective on life and you will learn how to appreciate the small things that you used to take for granted. I'm confident that you will be absolutely fine—*soon*.

I can't wait to meet the new you.

I can't wait to meet you when the storm is over. I can't wait to meet the person you will become. The resilient person you will become; how caring and giving you will be, how soft yet strong you will be, how wise and helpful you will be and how you will transform your life. I can't wait for you to change your life. I can't wait to see you living the life you always wanted to live. I know it will get better because *you* will be better and you will look back at this time and barely remember this feeling.

23

When You Start Turning Your Sadness Into Something Better

Lauren Evans

No longer am I going to let sadness take over my brain, take over my actions, or take over my day. What happened to me wasn't my fault, no matter what some people say. I know the arguments—if I hadn't taken the photos in the first place, none of this would have happened. But that isn't helpful thinking or any sort of advice, that's just an invalid opinion. My mind is tired of blame.

A lot of people take naked selfies of themselves without any repercussions—just like it should be. It is not my fault that somebody I trusted betrayed me by sharing something so intimate with one of the most creepy corners of the internet that I've ever had the misfortune to see. My photos should never have been shared without my permission. Each naked selfie, in fact, any sort of selfie, is the property of the person who took the photo, and it is theirs alone. That is the end argument. The person that betrays that trust is the one in the wrong.

I am not to blame.

Some said that I was stupid to trust somebody with such photos and that the punishment I got was what I deserved. The sadness I felt made me believe that was true. I was being deservedly punished for being 'promiscuous', for not being 'ladylike' and for 'lacking any decency and self-respect'. Sure, I've questioned my self-respect a few times when reflecting on how I have let men treat me, or how my body dysmorphic disorder has unknowing trained my brain to need adoration in order to feel better about my appearance. I've decided though that these destructive thoughts aren't going to drown me anymore.

My actions were not wrong. I wasn't wrong to take photos of myself. I wasn't wrong to think that I could trust somebody I had been friends with for over 6 years.

In a society where an unwanted dick pic can be justified with 'boys will be boys' or 'it's just banter', my naked selfies are nothing to be ashamed of. I'm not going to take that supposed deserved punishment from anybody, especially myself. Whatever is thrown at me from others or from my own sense of guilt, it won't make me sad anymore.
I'm not in the wrong.

Guilt is my strongest emotion. It can make me curl up in a ball, turn into a shell of what I once was, and make me avoid all human contact. It makes me feel like half a person. It takes my worth away from me. Nobody can make me feel worse than me. I am the master at it. The power of guilt and self-blame inside me beats any comments from other people.

They can try and put me down, but they won't win.

They'll nudge me in that direction—sticks and stones and all that—but ultimately, my downward spiral is controlled only by the powers of my feelings of guilt and my feelings of sadness, and that is my brain's doing, nobody else's.

When you have imagined yourself bleeding out in a bathtub or jumping out of a third-story window to crush your skull, there isn't much lower you can go. Nobody made me feel like that—I did.

I blamed myself for what happened for months. Depression took hold of me and quickly dragged me down, deeper than I ever imagined depression could take somebody. I stopped seeing friends from the shame of just being depressed, let alone what happened to me. I stopped going to work. I stopped getting out of bed. I stopped imagining a future for myself. All possible futures had gone—all dream lives dissolved. The only thing I could picture what my suicide.

And guess what emotion stopped from being a danger to myself? Yep. Guilt has saved the life that it had tried to destroy. I thought about the horror of somebody I care about finding me. I thought about the upset of my family, the broken heart of my boyfriend. So I did nothing. Guilt lead the way once again, and though I felt pathetic to not have the 'courage' to go through with anything, I also felt pathetic for thinking about death in the first place.

However many times I'm told to try and not think about what happened, I know that though the advice comes from a supportive place, it's not realistic. Sure, over time I'll think about it less. It's been almost 10 months now and I am thinking about it less. Though that time has passed, it still takes hold of me and controls my day. I still have to hide under the safety of the bed covers for hours, my thoughts spiraling out of control until I am numb.

That sadness isn't going to have that power anymore. I'm not going to cry about it anymore. I'm going to get angry instead.

I'll throw paint at a canvas and hang it on the wall. I'll turn the real-life villain into a victim in an award-winning piece of fiction. I'll use the anger to run for miles. I'll beat chicken breasts with a rolling pin and enjoy the tasty results. I'll turn it into a personal essay that helps others going through a similar experience. I'm going to use the emotions and make something good. I'm going to embrace the anger, and no doubt some sadness, and imagine the villains from before being hurt each time I keep on going with my life. Like a voodoo doll, every time I ignore victim-shaming comments or avoid self-shaming thoughts, those enemies will feel a sharp pain in their sides.

I will keep living my life how I want to live it—helping others and writing great things. And nobody can stop me, especially those that try to make me feel bad about myself, or those who have tried to hurt me by betraying my trust. I won't let them or myself get in my way.

I'm going to keep being honest and open about what happened, because whatever a hater says about it, I have thought worse. But from now on, I'm going to think better.

24

An Unedited Conversation With My Depression And Anxiety

Kelli Rose

I can think of about 800 things that I need to be doing right now but my old friends Anxiety and Depression unexpectedly came home to visit. They're not the kind of guests that you would enjoy having over because they demand all of your undivided attention. They're the kind of guests that come in, take over and dictate your entire schedule for the remainder of their stay. They don't give a certain date of their departure, so you must prepare to be in it for the long haul.

I'm supposed to be cleaning and packing for our move this weekend but Anxiety says I don't have enough time to do everything before Saturday, so what's the point in doing anything at all? Depression is reminding me how much I love this house and how badly I don't want to leave, so she's telling me that I should sit right here in this chair because I won't be able to sit in this room for much longer.

I know I have a lot left to do at the new house to get ready, so I need to get things taken care of here first but Anxiety says there's too much on my to-do list so I need to rethink all of it before I begin. I need to start organizing things to pack but I don't have enough boxes for everything yet, so Anxiety says I should wait until I have them all together. I have a mountain of clothes that need to be washed and stored away, but Anxiety says that there's too much to get done so Depression suggests that I put it off for another day.

My boyfriend is working long hours a few cities away, so Depression is telling me that I am incapable of doing all of this stuff by myself. During our last move, I was surrounded by friends and family offering helping hands to get everything done. This time I'm almost two hours away and have to handle it on my own, but Depression tells me that if they really cared, they would've come to help me anyway. Anxiety chimes in and reminds me that they've probably talked about this among themselves, and they think it's entertaining to see how well I do under this kind of pressure. Depression agrees and says that if I don't try, then I won't fail. Anxiety nods but reminds me that I'll fail anyway regardless of what I decide to do. Here is where I settle between my rock and my hard place.

I'll likely stay here for the remainder of my day, fighting with these demons that perch on each of my shoulders. When my boyfriend gets home and nothing is done, he'll have questions for me that I don't have answers to, because he doesn't hear the voices like I do. He doesn't understand how these conclusions are formed. He'll be frustrated and agitated by my existence and lack of motivation, but he won't understand that I am, too. He'll tell me that he doesn't get why everything always has to fall on him, but he doesn't see the weight that bears heavy on my shoulders. He'll storm away, leaving me to hear the bitter words of, "I told you so," by Anxiety and Depression once again.

They're the only ones that never leave me.

25

17 Things You Learn The Year After Being Diagnosed With Depression

Katie Mather

1. It's ok. You're ok.

2. It's comforting to know that your behavior in the past however many years of your life can be explained by a dopamine defect.

3. There are some people who react and behave exactly as you worried they would. They'll tell you to exercise more, to eat more greens. They'll advise that you simply should get over it—that these ~*~blue feelings~*~ will pass.

4. You'll learn not to listen to them.

5. There are some people (unfortunately the population of which is incredibly minute) who really, really understand.

6. You don't want to be an emotional burden on anybody, but these people who *get it* should be featured in your life for forever.

7. You'll learn what's really important to keep in mind is that people will still love you.

8. Medication doesn't mean you're one breakdown away from being sent to an American Horror Story-style asylum. It helps. It's supposed to help.

9. And you're not weak. You definitely feel that way, but you're not.

10. You're allowed to stay a full day in bed without feeling like a failure. Even if you don't brush your teeth.

11. A hot shower doesn't permanently fix anything, but it's a necessary comfort.

12. Food is not a permanent solution or escape.

13. Meticulous lists will save your head from imploding. Even if the list consists of "Get out of bed" or "Wash hair," you'll learn how powerful the feeling of physically crossing things off is to your mental state.

14. Good days are really good days. But sometimes you'll spend a little too much time stressing over when the good feelings will end. It takes a while to overcome that mindset and just accept what's happening here and now.

15. You'll eventually find something that helps you cope.

You'll fill every minute of the day with activity so you can't stop and think. You'll accept (and actually go to) every social event invitation you receive on Facebook. You'll go to the gym every other day. You figure it out.

16. After accepting yourself as someone with a "mental illness," it's freeing. You're no longer in denial. You know and understand the way you are and now you can work with it.

17. A year can change a lot.

26

You Might Not Be Okay Today, But Some Day You Will Be

Lorie Abing

Like a thief into the night, memories you wish you'd forget would slip into your mind, when your guard is at its lowest.

And then it hits you all at once—like slamming into a brick wall, walking barefoot on broken shards of glass, freezing on a stormy December night.

There are days when even getting yourself out of bed seems like a daunting task. Why bother when you know in the middle of the afternoon you're going to have to get a hold of yourself—close your eyes, count to ten, and breathe deeply—anything just keep your emotions in check because the flashbacks come at the most unfortunate moments, when you're surrounded by people who have no idea what you're going through, and that you'd rather keep it that way.

And then there are days when you feel absolutely nothing. Nothing and no one seems to be of interest. Existing, but not living. Functional but without purpose, save for the sake of having something to do. Maybe it's because you cried too hard last night that you used up all your emotional coupons for the week. Or that your self-esteem ran too low, like a well that's close to drying up. Or you're just exhausted, from feeling every emotion from the chain of memories that one small link sets off.

No, you don't want to be a walking contradiction of a lifeless living.

As tempting as the path to numbness sounds, the ice cold personality that comes with it, and the promise of indifference to pain and heartbreak, I hope you still choose to feel.

Loss, failure, misery. They make you want to shut down your emotions. But what about hope, success, happiness, gratitude, and love? Wouldn't those outweigh everything else?

And there will be days when you feel like you can take on anything that the world will throw at you. I hope these are the days you have more of. You force yourself to go back to your definition of normal—to do the things you usually do, the food you usually eat, the books you usually read, the friends you usually talk to, the places you usually go to, the work you usually do.

You're not okay—you're sad. Broken, even. But that doesn't mean you should put your life on hold.

Don't let the negativity cripple you. There's always a bright side. Always.

Little by little, step by step, you carve your path back to happiness. How empowering it is that you have that choice and that it is yours and yours alone to make; taking that choice to move forward is already an accomplishment no one could take away from you.

Never ever discredit yourself. Even if you have those days when you want to succumb to the sadness and let time pass lying in bed, or those days when you want to lock all your emotions and throw away the key, don't think of it as a step backward. Let it be just roadblocks—you're still moving forward, just on a rockier path.

As one of the sayings I firmly believe in goes,

> "The only time you should ever look back is to see how far you've come."
>
> —Anonymous

Eventually, the brick wall seemed will crack, the shards crushed into finer pieces, the storm reduced to a drizzle.

You're getting there, and you're coming out stronger in the aspects that matter the most to you and to everyone who cares about you.

It gets better, in time.

27

Read This If It Feels Like Your Depression Is Getting The Best Of You

Kendra Syrdal

Around you, the sun keeps rising and setting. The traffic keeps pressing through in the most unrelenting way. The clouds roll by, the holidays happen. Everyone talks about how they can't believe October is over and winter is almost here. And you smile behind steaming cider as if you're just excited as them.

But really, if you were being truly honest, you'd admit that nothing has felt different since August. Rather everything feels blurry, muffled. You've lost track of the days and the nights because instead of being individual sunrises and sunsets, it's just another day of you feeling like you're walking upstream against a raging current. And instead of fighting, instead of it feeling like a challenge, you're just getting tired.

Too many times you've just laid in bed avoiding any and every responsibility. You don't know when the last time you checked your mail was. It's probably overflowing with unanswered letters from cable companies (thank god for automatic withdrawal) and catalogs filled with girls who had enough energy to wash their hair that morning. You sit in the tub watching the now lukewarm water draining beneath you and you wish for a second that you'd go down with it into some abyss where there are not problems outside of wondering where the end of the pipe will take you.

The stereotypical depressed person is always in the dark maybe with ugly, forlorn, black, mascara streaks painting her cheeks or maybe staring with his bloodshot, red eyes from popping vessels while sobbing. And they sit alone, still in the dark, with that unnecessary war paint, contemplating how much better the world would be without them. And even though that's a stereotype, sometimes that monster comes in rearing it's nasty head and messes everything up.

As terrible as the extreme depression, the scary feeling of doom that exists, more often than not, it's a different monster. And it's a monster that doesn't exist in the crazy highs or lows and because of that; it isn't as easy to spot. It hangs out in the corners undetected just waiting until it can latch on and never let go.

Depression sometimes is a feeling of utter desolation, but what about when it isn't?

uote">Sarah Silverman recently described depression as the feeling of homesickness, but you're home so there's no way to satiate the feeling. I couldn't agree or relate more. It's knowing you have no real reason to not be ecstatic, to not be happy, but instead of feeling anything all you can feel is unenthused, sulky, static.

It's seeing all of the crayons laid out in front of you, the entire 120-count Crayola box you always coveted in grade school, every single color you could possibly imagine. It's seeing them and having the ability to pick any color, but only being able to force yourself back to the same broken gray crayon day after day after day.

It's watching people promote asinine things like "drinking more tea" and "running for the endorphins" and thinking, "Fine. I'll give it a fucking shot." But then your bladder is bursting from your 18th cup of stupid chamomile and your shins are aching from running for hours, but even after heeding all of this naturopathic bullshit you still just want to sit on the kitchen floor and eventually blend into your surroundings, ceasing to be you because being you is getting exhausting.

It's hearing about how Prozac changed someone's life and how therapy is their everything, so you keep popping open the little orange bottle and talking about your ex-best friend and your fears every Thursday. You do all of the things you're supposed to do but nothing's different. It's researching at 4 AM for any possible answer but still not wanting to smile at jokes on Twitter or text anyone back because you just suck. And if you know it they must know it too.

It's feeling like the same bland, sad, murky version of yourself day after day and just wondering if this is how the rest of your life will be.

So even though you got up this morning and you felt the like nothing was different, you feel like you've accepted that you will never have highs again, you still feel like you're looking through fogged up glasses, and you're simply going through the motions, there's one thing to keep in mind.

You did get up.

And even though your world right now is that broken gray, your vision is clouded, you homesickness has not been relieved, and you're choking down more fucking tea to try and "naturally cure yourself", one day it won't feel that way. It might not be tomorrow, or next month, but eventually, it will be one day. That day your eyes will be clear, your heart won't be heavy, and you'll find yourself reaching for an orange or a green while you order a coffee because why not.

You just have to keep getting up.

28

If You Need To Believe One Thing, Believe That You Are Loved

Alexandria Brown

Hi. My name is Alexandria and I have depression, anxiety, a touch of OCD and a whole lot of quirks. I hate saying those words out loud and admitting that I have some cracks in my armor. I have a good life going for me but I struggle on a regular basis to see the good in things, which makes me a hypocrite because I speak about happiness and why people should be happy on a regular basis. I do truly believe that but internally my brain is at war with itself.

So this one is for you. The person keeping it together when really you feel like falling apart. And you, the person who looks like they have everything and knows they have a ton to be grateful for but just can't. Or you, the person who just feels incredibly alone right now.

I get it. I've been there. I've looked at myself and thought about how easy it would be to just not exist. I wouldn't be in pain. I would lift the burden from my family and friends. I would be able to just not anymore.

But then I thought about it. That's what my anxiety wants. That's what my depression wants. The terrible two want me to give up on myself and just succumb to the darkness. And I didn't come to this realization alone. I have been in therapy for a long time. Dealing with the dark things that have been haunting me for a while.

I was tired of my friends and family telling me I was fine. I knew that they just wanted me to be happy but unfortunately, unless you've been through this, it's hard to really explain to people.

So I get you. I get where you're coming from right now. You're wanting to know if there's a light at the other end of the tunnel. If there's something good coming around the corner to make all this bad seem like it wasn't that bad. You want to know that if you get through this one more time that the pain and the down cycle might just leave you alone for good.

I wish I could tell you that it does. That magically you end up better and that you can go on feeling happy for the rest of your life. I can't because that's not true. You're going to go through tough shit. You're going to deal with hardship. But you can fight your way through it. I mean you've gotten through all the hard times so far, so you're already ahead of the game.

I want you to know one thing; you are so loved.

Maybe you don't see it right now. I know it definitely doesn't feel like it but you are. There is someone who loves you and wants you to be OK. They want to make sure you're around to see another day. Maybe they don't fully understand what you're going through but if they're there in the dark times then they're the kind of people you keep around.

Those people are the ones who hold you tightly as your panic attack starts to set in. The ones who talk you through the bad times. The ones who lay next to you in your bed when you can't get out from under the covers. Even if they physically can't be there, if you have someone just checking in on you no matter distance, then those people are amazing. Hold on to those people.

And when it feels like you have nothing or no one, just remember one thing; you are loved. Try not to question that. Just keep that in the back of your mind when everything life starts to get harder. You are loved.

29

A Love Letter To My Anti-Depressant

Ari Eastman

You met me at a very strange time in my life. Shit, I just accidentally quoted *Fight Club*, didn't I? I'm suddenly every bro posing with a tiger on Tinder I've ever made fun of. Nothing against Chuck Palahniuk, but you know, read another book maybe? You can't ALL love *Fight Club* that much…right?

Whatever, I digress.

You first came into my world when I was fourteen, which we can both agree is a disgustingly awkward age. I was overzealous with tweezers, plucking about half my eyebrows completely off, and still wearing a heavy amount of under-eye black liner. I was fighting insomnia, acid reflux, and the nagging feeling that I was going to die. Every. Single. Night.

Anxiety is a huge dick like that. And not in a good way.

It shows up without any real reason. Dumb things would set me off, like my father driving over a bridge, my teacher mentioning the 1906 earthquake, or just sitting alone long enough that my panicked thoughts took over. Everything seemed designed to kill me. That's what anxiety does, convinces you *everything* is a threat.

I'd been struggling for two years prior, but it was now at the point that we were seeking medicinal help. Nobody wants to medicate their fourteen year old. But nobody wants a fourteen year old suffering from constant panic attacks either.

And in walked a small baby blue pill. Zoloft. A relationship that would blossom in a way I never could have expected. My longest commitment. A love story people will write about in history books one day, I like to think.

Hey, Z. I should have written you a long time ago. I don't know if you realize my deep appreciation. I know, there have been times I was rash and thought I was fine without you. I looked into alternative options. I ran away with boys and thought oxytocin was enough. I didn't want you to be the most serious relationship I ever had. I wanted to prove to myself I didn't need you.

But time and time again, I wound up begging at your doorstep. When my anxiety decided to invite depression along, you were there. I was driving close to cliffs asking you to see me again. Z, I was foolish thinking you weren't part of me. I looked at it the wrong way. I saw you as a failure, as evidence of my incorrectly formed brain. I didn't want that. Can you understand that?

I wanted to see if I could exist without you.

And maybe one day, I can. I'm not sure. I'm not willing to make any bold statements either way.

Because all I know is each time I hit rock bottom, you sat there beaming in your bottle telling me it would be okay. You reminded me asking for help is not a sign of weakness. You told me the bravest thing I could ever do is take care of my mind, my body, my health. You came back and the demons weren't as terrifying anymore. They seemed doable.

With you, the hardships do not defeat me.

With you, I am resilient and brilliant and exactly who I was always meant to be. With you, I'm the best me.

Z, I love you for everything you've given me. Everything you've given back to me.

What a beautiful gift that is, to give me back the piece of myself that sometimes goes missing. How could I ever be ashamed of that? How could I ever be afraid to tell the world how utterly lovely you are?

Thank you.

30

How Depression Makes You Believe That Things Aren't Supposed To Go Well For You

Maya Kachroo-Levine

Depression taints some of your best moments.

It doesn't make you incapable of being happy for yourself, feeling proud or enjoying your success. But it quells your triumphs, or puts a more subdued smile on your face, because you're waiting for something to go wrong.

You're not even conscious of when it starts. Your mind is pushing too far ahead, and the inevitable *what ifs* seep into your head; an unwelcome set of irrational thoughts you're predisposed to have.

Think about the moment after joy. Something goes well, you get what you want. You have a few seconds of happiness, a celebratory drink, a moment of elation caught on Instagram. What happens after you feel excitement, extreme relief, or pride?

You don't think of the most immediate problem, you think about the most extreme one. A crucial sign of mental illness is an inability to differentiate the rational, logical conclusions from the irrational conclusions that are fueling your concern.

If you like what you're doing at work, you wonder what the catch is.

If you're in a new relationship, you can't help thinking about how bad the breakup would be.

If you move to the place of your dreams, you're too distracted by what you gave up to enjoy it.

If you come into money, you feel guilty.

You feel guilty for most of your happiness. You feel like you don't deserve it.

You do, of course. And if you could push the irrational fears away for long enough you'd see it, but you can't. Your instinct is to cling to the irrational fears, wrapping them around you like a blanket. It's impossible to let them go, because should anything go wrong your concerns will at least be validated as a consolation prize.

You know these fears are irrational but even when you repeat that truth back to yourself, it doesn't calm you. Internalizing those fears just makes them more real.

If you grew up with depression or shared a roof with a depressed parent, or sibling, you understand what it feels like to expect that things will go wrong. When you grow up with depression in your house, you come to see things going wrong as your norm.

It's not always a happy way to live. It's upsetting to always have your good news fall away with the panic that you'll fuck something up, or some unknown circumstance will take the good in your life. You try to remind yourself that you're in control, and nothing will go wrong. You're unconvinced.

Depression pushes you to assume that when something goes right for you, a wrong will even it out. The way people with OCD are with symmetry: That's you, and happiness. That's you, and all things good.

It's like being a glutton for punishment, but not in a Capulet/ Montague, moment before the kiss, type way. In a self-sabotaging way, that only people who don't understand a world without a mess on their hands know.

Sometimes you gravitate toward it because you know things will go awry, and will even occasionally lead them there as a defense mechanism. Like cheating on someone before they break up with you. Or never asking for something that might actually make you happy.

The notion that things could get better and then *stay better* is foreign to you. You're scared to say yes to a good thing because you have a sinking feeling that something else will go wrong as a result. And even when you know how much you deserve to have things go well, you're still scared to believe it.

Thought Catalog, it's a website.

www.thoughtcatalog.com

Social

facebook.com/thoughtcatalog
twitter.com/thoughtcatalog
tumblr.com/thoughtcatalog
instagram.com/thoughtcatalog

Corporate

www.thought.is

Made in United States
Troutdale, OR
07/22/2023

11477829R00094